Does a Ten-Gallon Hat Really Hold Ten Gallons?

And Other Questions about Fashion

ALISON BEHNKE

ILLUSTRATIONS BY **COLIN W. THOMPSON**

LERNER PUBLICATIONS COMPANY

Minneapolis

Contents

Perhaps you've heard these statements about fashion:

Less is more!
Thin is in!

But what's the story behind the statements? And is there any truth to them?

Come along with us as we explore different beliefs about fashion. Find out whether the things you may have heard about clothing, style, and trendy looks are

FACT OR FICTION!

Is It True That Women Once Wore Skirts So Wide They Could Barely Walk through Doors?

WELL, NOT QUITE. **But they did wear skirts wide enough that only one woman at a time could go through a doorway!**

In the mid-1800s, very full, wide skirts were all the rage in Europe and North America. Women who wore these skirts used various contraptions to make them the right shape. Hoops and cagelike frames helped women get the right look. Women also wore layer upon layer of crinolines (stiff petticoats).

As skirts got wider and wider, they became more and more difficult to manage. Women had to be careful not to get too near fireplaces for fear of their skirts going up in flames. Walking down a busy city street could be like going through an obstacle course. Getting into a horse-drawn carriage was no easy feat either. Simply sitting down could be such a challenge that "ladies' chairs" became popular. These special chairs had wide seats and no arms. They made it easier for women in wide skirts to sit down.

In the late 1800s and early 1900s, the trend swung from hoops to hobbles. Hobble skirts were very narrow at the bottom. Women could take only tiny steps (hobble) while wearing them.

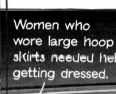

Women who wore large hoop skirts needed help getting dressed.

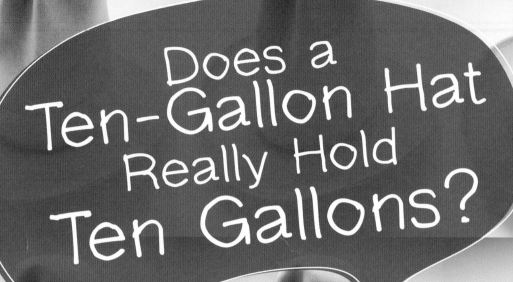

Does a Ten-Gallon Hat Really Hold Ten Gallons?

NOPE! Ten-gallon hats are big, but they ain't *that* big, pardner. The average ten-gallon hat can actually hold about 3 quarts (2.8 liters) of water. There are 4 quarts in 1 gallon (3.7 liters). That means a hat that really did hold 10 gallons (37 liters) would be more than thirteen times the size of a ten-gallon hat!

No one is exactly sure where these broad-brimmed, cowboy-style hats got their name. But a couple of theories suggest the name came from Spanish words.

In the 1800s, American and Mexican cowboys (called vaqueros) both herded cattle in Texas. (Texas did not become part of the United States until 1845.) Vaqueros wore hats that were similar to the American cowboy hats. They had braiding around the brim. The braiding was called galloon—or, in Spanish, *galón*. This might explain the "gallon" part of the name. But then where did the "ten" part of *ten-gallon hat* come from? That is still a mystery.

Another theory is that vaqueros might have called the Americans' hats *tan galán*, meaning "so gallant." (*Gallant* means "brave or heroic.") American cowboys who didn't know Spanish could have thought the phrase sounded like "ten gallon."

The cowboys probably would have liked being called brave and heroic! But most people who study the history of words think the other theory is more likely to be right. One thing is for sure: "three-quart hat" just doesn't have the same ring to it!

This cowboy lived in the United States in the 1800s.

Did Some Women Once Wear Corsets So Tight That They Damaged Their Bodies?

YES, THEY DID. Corsets are undergarments that shape the body. Women around the world have worn versions of the corset for thousands of years. Some historians think women in ancient Greece wore corsetlike garments in about 2000 B.C. But corsets really became popular in the Middle Ages (A.D. 500–1500). And the corset trend continued for decades after the Middle Ages had ended.

Corsets were probably never comfy. But they became downright dangerous between the mid-1800s and early 1900s. During this period, fashionable women in Europe and the United States wanted their waists to look very, very tiny. Even women who were already thin longed for skinnier middles. Cane, whalebone, wood, or metal gave corsets their shape and strength. And they were very strong indeed. They were usually so tight that women needed help getting them on. Often a maid yanked on the laces at the back of the corset. Meanwhile, the corseted lady held on to a bedpost or other sturdy object.

But while corsets gave women the shape they wanted, they could do damage. At the least, they often caused back pain. And very tight corsets could squeeze internal organs, pushing them out of place inside the body. Some may have even cracked or damaged women's ribs.

Corsets also made it hard to breathe. They could cause fainting. To avoid passing out in the middle of a party—how embarrassing!—ladies carried smelling salts. Smelling salts were a combination of chemicals and perfume. Sniffing them helped revive women who felt faint and kept them from tumbling into the punch bowl from a lack of oxygen.

Did You Know?

Rumors once went around that some ladies in the 1800s had a few ribs removed for fashion. The missing ribs would have allowed them to wear even tighter corsets and have even slimmer waists. But historians think these rumors are false. Such surgery would have been incredibly painful—and probably fatal.

Has Thin Always Been In?

A group of women exercise in a 1980s aerobics class. In the 1980s, thin was in—but it hasn't always been the fashion.

NO! Throughout history, society and politics have affected what type of body is fashionable. It has varied from era to era and nation to nation.

During many periods, a plumper figure was stylish for both men and women. It showed that the person had enough money to eat well. It could also mean that the person was wealthy enough not to do physical labor.

There are also biological reasons for preferring a bigger build. For a woman, a curvy figure suggests that she would easily be able to have children.

In the 1920s, a thinner physique came into vogue in the United States and Europe. World War I (1914–1918) had been a terrible time. Millions of young men died. After the war, young people wanted to break loose and have fun. They longed for carefree times. People began to associate fashion and fun with youth—and thinness.

In the 1980s, being thin became even more fashionable. Once again, style reflected society to some degree. People who had lots of time and money could go to expensive gyms. They could hire personal trainers to help them keep fit.

In the 2000s, slim physiques remain in fashion. But being too thin is just as unhealthful as being overweight. Eating disorders such as anorexia and bulimia are very dangerous.

Sunny Styles

Like trends about body size, the fashion for suntans has social history. Centuries ago, suntanned skin showed that a person worked outside and probably did not make much money. Most wealthy people had paler skin. But later, suntans became linked to the luxury of going on tropical vacations—or to a tanning parlor. Doctors have learned that suntanning can be bad for your health, however. So suntans have slowly started to fall out of fashion.

Did Women Once Paint Their Legs Instead of Wearing Stockings?

YES! BUT NOT BECAUSE THEY WERE FEELING ARTSY.
During World War II (1939–1945), the United States and some European nations rationed (limited) goods. This meant most people couldn't have the luxuries they had before the war. And it seriously cramped the style of many women.

Women get their legs painted at a department store in London in 1941.

Stockings were a rationed item. At that time, they were made of silk or nylon. Silk was very expensive. And nylon was needed for the war. For example, many parachutes were made of nylon. So people didn't want to waste the material on less important goods—like stockings.

Faced with this fashion challenge, some women took a creative approach. They painted the skin of their legs to look as though they were wearing stockings!

Shops offered products to help women with this project. Drugstores sold powders to mix with water and use as paint. Women who could not afford these goods made their own concoctions. They made mixtures out of household staples such as flour, starch, and water.

The color wasn't the only challenge. Stockings at that time had seams up the back of each leg. So many women used makeup pencils to draw lines on their calves. Or to make things much easier, they had a relative or friend help!

Out with the Old, In with the New

Stockings weren't the only clothing item affected by rationing. Laws limited the amount of fabric in skirts and pants too. But after the war, in 1947, a French designer named Christian Dior introduced a new fashion line. Nicknamed the New Look, it was very controversial. Dior's look included full skirts that used lots and lots of fabric. His clothes were fancy and romantic. People were still reeling from the war's tragedies. Many thought Dior's luxurious line was inappropriate. Even so, Dior became one of Europe's best-known designers.

Is Makeup Bad for You?

NOT USUALLY. Some people are allergic to ingredients in some cosmetics. But scientists test most modern makeup to make sure that it is safe.

In the past, however, makeup could be very dangerous indeed. In ancient Egypt, fashionable men and women both wore heavy eye makeup. They outlined their eyes in dark colors and put colored shadow on the eyelids. Some of their makeup included lead. This metal is poisonous to people. As it builds up in the body, it can cause tiredness, weakness, memory loss, and even death.

But ancient peoples didn't know about lead's dangers. The ancient Romans also used it in makeup. Romans found pale skin attractive. Women lightened their faces with powders containing white lead. Some women died of lead poisoning. Yet in sixteenth-century Europe, ladies were still powdering their noses (and cheeks and foreheads and necks) with lead-based makeup.

Also during the 1500s, England's Queen Elizabeth I made red hair all the rage. Women dyed their hair and wigs the fashionable color. Some dyes contained sulfur and lead. They could cause upset stomachs, headaches, and nosebleeds.

In the 1800s, some makeup contained arsenic, a poisonous chemical. And in the following century, many women still went to painful lengths for beauty.

Hollywood movie stars helped make blonde hair wildly stylish. Eager for the same look, many American women bleached (took the color out of) their hair. They used chemicals called peroxide and ammonia. Bleaching could lead to headaches, burned scalps, and hair loss.

Marilyn Monroe helped make bleached blonde hair popular in the 1950s.

Are Tattoos Must-Have Body Decorations in Some Cultures?

YES! New Zealand's Maori people have been tattooing their bodies for centuries. They have intricate tattoos on their faces.

This Maori warrior has traditional tattoos on his face.

Tattoos like this one are common in many countries and cultures. But in some cultures, tattoos have specific meanings.

Tattoos can also mark people as members of certain groups. For example, the yakuza is a centuries-old organized crime group in Japan. Since about the 1600s, many yakuza members have decorated their bodies with colorful tattoos. These tattoos often cover most of the body. Sometimes they resemble armor. The wives and daughters of yakuza members sometimes have tattoos as well. These tattoos show the women's loyalty to their family and to the group.

Traditionally, Maori men and women have both had facial tattoos. Men's tattoos are larger and more detailed, however. These tattoos are a bit like identity cards. Their patterns and placement show information about a person's social status, family, and even what work they do.

Tattoos have also had specific meaning in other cultures. Eighteenth-century British sailors visited Tahiti, an island in the South Pacific Ocean. They saw that many people there had tattoos and soon adopted the practice themselves. Sailors' tattoos meant certain things. For example, an image of a swallow traditionally meant that the sailor had traveled 5,000 nautical miles (5,754 miles, or 9,260 kilometers). Other tattoos were based on superstitions. A pig and a rooster on each calf, ankle, or foot supposedly protected a sailor from drowning.

A retired Japanese yakuza crime boss shows the tattoos on his back.

Has Less (Clothing) Always Been More (Fashionable)?

Beachgoers in Mobile, Alabama, in 1900 model their modest swimwear.

DEFINITELY NOT. In some eras and countries, it has been taboo (against custom) for women, in particular, to show very much of their bodies. For example, in the 1800s, European women wore bathing outfits that covered everything but their heads, hands, and feet. One hundred years later, bathing suits still went to the elbows and knees. In Chicago in 1921, some women had to pay fines for showing their bare arms!

Over time, however, social norms changed. During World War II, when fabric was rationed, skirts got shorter. Later, in 1960s America, the fight for equal rights was going strong. Women were part of that fight. In the 1960s, women were expected to marry and raise children. Most women didn't work outside the home. Women thought they should have more freedom to make choices. As they gained more freedom, they also adopted a freer style of dress. Hemlines went up—way up. Women wore shorter skirts than ever before.

Fashion dos and don'ts can also vary depending on the local weather. In many hot African, Asian, and Caribbean nations, less clothing— for men *and* women—has always been in style. Australian aborigines (native people) also have a dress code calling for little coverage.

Religion can play a role too. Some Muslims (people who follow the religion of Islam) believe that women should cover almost their whole bodies— including their faces—in public. Some Jews believe that married women must cover their hair in public. Amish women wear dresses with long skirts and long sleeves.

A Muslim woman covers her face and body with an abaya (full-length robe).

Who Wears the Pants?

Social codes about dressing aren't always about coverage. For centuries, it was taboo for women in much of the world to wear pants. One of the first American women to try to make pants stylish for ladies was Victoria Woodhull. She was also the first American woman to run for president, in 1872. Woodhull said that once she was elected, she would wear pants in the White House. She did not win the presidency, so no one knows if her fashion sense would have taken the country by storm!

Are Brides Always All Dressed in White?

NOT AT ALL! In many countries, brides wear very colorful outfits. And even in countries where brides currently wear white, white weddings have not always been in fashion.

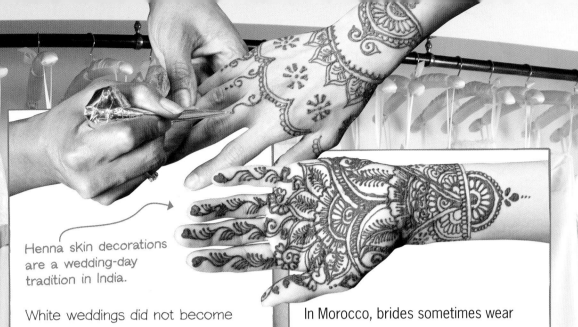

Henna skin decorations are a wedding-day tradition in India.

White weddings did not become trendy in Europe until the 1800s. Before this time, women often wore blue, red, or nearly whatever color they liked to their weddings. But in 1840, Britain's Queen Victoria got married in a beautiful white gown. The dress caught the attention of women in Britain and beyond. Soon many brides had adopted the custom of wearing white.

In other parts of the world, women follow their own wedding-dress customs. In China, many women wear red on their wedding day. In Chinese culture, this color stands for good fortune. In Norway, on the other hand, green is a traditionally lucky color. Some Norwegian brides also wear a traditional bridal crown.

In Morocco, brides sometimes wear green, but yellow is also common. Moroccans believe yellow keeps away bad luck. In some other African nations, wedding-day wear depends on where the couple is from. Different villages, towns, and regions often have patterns or colors associated with them.

In India, many women choose saris (traditional Indian gowns) in red and white for their weddings. An Indian bride's female family members also decorate her hands and feet with designs. They use a temporary dye called henna.

Blue is a lucky wedding-day color in Ireland. And in Scotland, many women include their family tartan in their wedding outfit. Tartans are plaid patterns representing Scottish family groups called clans.

Were Fashionable Men Once Called Macaroni?

YES! In the mid to late 1700s, a group of young British men began wearing fancy and rather outrageous outfits. These men were nicknamed macaroni.

In this late 1700s cartoon, the man on the right models macaroni fashions while his father expresses dismay.

Just like the pasta, this name came from Italy. A few hundred years ago, most young, wealthy British men went on months-long European trips as part of their education. This vacation was called the grand tour. It almost always included time in Italy and France. In the eighteenth century, some of these travelers adopted French and Italian fashions. They took their new looks home to Britain with them.

Favorite macaroni fashion choices included very tall wigs. Some reports said that a macaroni's hairdo could tower up to 18 inches (45 centimeters) above his head! The macaronis also wore high-heeled shoes, colorful stockings, and tightly fitted jackets.

Not everyone liked the macaroni look. Some older British people thought it was silly. Some newspaper cartoonists drew pictures mocking the wild styles.

The macaroni men also show up in the eighteenth-century British song "Yankee Doodle." The song had many versions over the years, but one verse went like this:

> *Yankee Doodle went to town,*
> *A-Riding on a pony;*
> *He stuck a feather in his cap,*
> *And called it macaroni.*

The little tune became popular in the young United States. But the British had meant it as an insult! The song was saying that U.S. soldiers had no style. It said they were so tacky that they thought a few feathers in their hats could make them as fashionable as British macaroni.

"Yankee Doodle" sheet music from 1775

Did Chinese Women Once Bind Their Feet to Be Only a Few Inches Long?

YES. Beginning in about A.D. 900 or 1000, some Chinese women began tightly wrapping their feet. They wanted to make them smaller—much smaller. The practice seems to have come from an emperor who fell in love with a dancer who bound her feet.

The ideal size for a foot was just 3 inches (7 cm) long. To reach this goal, young girls went through a long and painful process. Tight bandages bound their feet into sharp arches. They bent the pinky toe underneath the foot, toward the heel. The bandages bent and broke some of the bones in the foot. In addition, the skin under the bandages sometimes rotted. Many girls died of infection.

Why did so many girls suffer this way? Was it for beauty alone? No. Over time, foot binding became very culturally important. Many girls and young women could not find husbands unless they had bound feet. For Chinese women, not getting married could mean a lifetime of poverty and hard work.

The Chinese government banned foot binding in 1912. But in some parts of China, the practice continued for several more decades. Some elderly women in modern China still have trouble walking because of their bound feet.

Did You Know?

Most poor Chinese women did not bind their feet. Their families needed their help in the fields and around the home. Bound feet would have made it too hard for them to do this work. But wealthier women did not have to do physical work. And they had servants to help them get around, since even walking was painful and difficult.

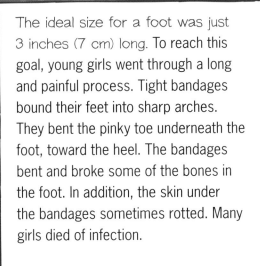

This image from the 1800s shows a young Chinese girl binding her feet.

Did a Dog Help Invent Velcro?

WELL . . . NOT EXACTLY. But a dog did provide the inspiration!

In the 1940s, a Swiss engineer named George de Mestral took a hunting trip in the mountains. He took his dog with him. One evening after a day walking through fields and woods, de Mestral noticed burrs sticking to his dog's fur. He also noticed that, though small, these burrs were strong. It was hard to remove them from the dog's coat.

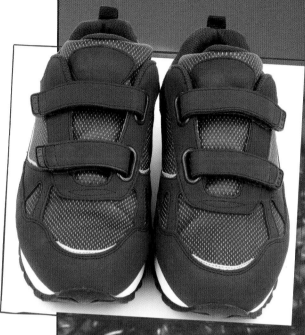

De Mestral took a closer look at the burrs. He saw that the plant seeds were covered with tiny, hooked spines. These hooks grabbed on to the hairs of the dog's coat. De Mestral wondered if he could create a fastener using the same hook-and-loop idea. It took time and patience—but he did it! He named his invention Velcro. The name came from the French words *velours* (meaning "velvet") and *crochet* (meaning "hook").

Velcro has had many uses in science, medicine, and even space exploration. But it's also a style staple. Its most famous fashion use is fastening shoes. It's quicker and easier than shoelaces—and noisier too!

It's also used to close many wallets. Some designers have used Velcro in bracelets, coats, backpacks, and more.

For his very helpful invention, de Mestral eventually became part of the U.S. National Inventors Hall of Fame. His dog, however, never got much credit.

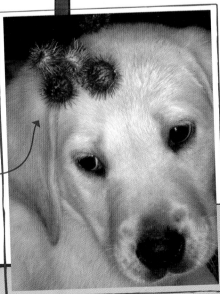

Burrs like these stuck in de Mestral's dog's fur, giving de Mestral the idea for Velcro.

Will Wearing a Hat Indoors Make You Go Bald?

NOPE! This rumor was once common. People warned that men who didn't remove their hats when entering buildings would lose their hair. But it's just not true.

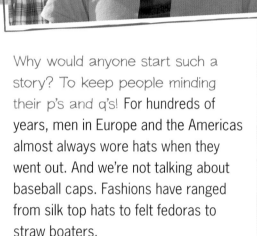

Why would anyone start such a story? To keep people minding their p's and q's! For hundreds of years, men in Europe and the Americas almost always wore hats when they went out. And we're not talking about baseball caps. Fashions have ranged from silk top hats to felt fedoras to straw boaters.

But while a fashionable man would never be caught without his hat *outside*, it was rude to wear it inside. So the rumor began that poor manners would be punished with hair loss!

Hats are no longer a fashion must. They fell out of style in about the 1960s. Over the years, fashions had become less formal. Young people, especially, were embracing freer ways of dressing. Many people simply thought hats were . . . well . . . old hat!

Were There Really 30-Inch-Tall Shoes?

AMAZINGLY, YES! In the 1500s, some wealthy women in Venice, Italy, wore platform shoes called chopines. The lowest chopines were about 6 inches (15 cm) high. But some soared to more than 2 feet (0.6 meters) tall! Women in these towering shoes needed servants to help them totter around the city.

Shoes are one of the most varied of all fashion items. And they have often blended function with fashion. Ancient Romans and Greeks lived in a warm, dry climate. They wore sandals that kept their feet cool. Most people living in the hottest parts of Africa have preferred similarly open shoes.

These girls from Holland are wearing klompen to keep their feet dry.

In Holland, beginning in about the 1200s, people wore *klompen*. These clunky wooden shoes kept feet dry in a wet country.

Less practical shoes have included *poulaines* (also called *crackows*). Men in fourteenth- and fifteenth-century Europe wore these shoes. They had long, pointy toes. Some poulaines were 18 inches (45 cm) long! Men had to stuff the points with wool, moss, or other fillers to keep the proper shape.

Shoes are also status symbols.
For example, much of India is very warm. Traditionally, most people there went barefoot much of the time.

So historically, only wealthy and high-status Indian people wore shoes. Shoes showed wealth in North America too. In the 1600s and beyond, some Native Americans traditionally wore moccasins. These leather, slipperlike shoes were usually pretty simple. They were tough, quiet, and easy to walk in. But some had decorated, beaded soles. They showed that the wearer was well-off enough to afford horses. Therefore, he did not have to walk from place to place—and could indulge in fancy shoes.

Are Supermodels *Really* Super?

Well, they can't leap tall buildings in a single bound. And they don't stop speeding trains with their bare hands. **BUT TO FASHION DESIGNERS, SUPERMODELS DO HAVE SPECIAL POWERS.** Designers depend on models to make their clothes look fabulous.

Models advertise fashions in magazines. They show off the latest styles on billboards. And runway models strut their stuff on catwalks in the globe's fashion capitals. For many years, the most important cities in the fashion world have been New York City, Paris, Milan, and London. In more recent times, other cities have also become important. They include Tokyo, Japan; São Paulo, Brazil; and Mumbai, India. Runway shows in these cities are a big deal. Fashion critics, shop owners, movie stars, and other potential customers all show up to see a designer's newest collection.

Most clothes in these shows are haute couture. *Haute couture* means "high sewing" in French. It refers to high-quality fashion design. Sometimes haute couture pieces are one of a kind.

These clothes would not fit an average person, but supermodels can make them work. Most designers prefer tall, thin models. The designers feel their clothes look best on this body type. In addition, some haute couture clothing is downright difficult to wear. It might include complicated skirts or superhigh collars. Often designers do not really make these pieces to be worn anywhere but on the runway or in photographs. These fancy garments are more like pieces of art than clothing.

As well as showing off a designer's clothes, models sometimes inspire designers' work. Many fashion designers have found muses (sources of creative inspiration) among their models.

Did You Know?

The average female model in the United States is about 5 feet 10 inches (1.8 m) tall and weighs less than 125 pounds (56 kilograms). By contrast, the average non-model American woman is about 5 feet 4 inches (1.6 m) tall and weighs more than 130 pounds (59 kg). Many models are thinner than is healthy.

Were Cowboys the First to Wear Jeans?

NO SIREE! In modern times, lots of people wear jeans nearly every day. They can be casual and comfortable or stylish and high fashion. But originally, they were simply sturdy work clothes.

Levi Strauss founded the first company to make jeans. Strauss was a German immigrant to the United States. In the 1850s, he sold fabric and other goods in California. In about 1860, he began making pants out of the sturdy French fabric *serge de Nimes*—or, as it later became known, denim.

Strauss was not the first person to make pants out of denim. In fact, the word *jeans* probably came from the denim trousers that sailors from Genoa, Italy, wore. In French, these pants were called *bleu de Gênes*. But with the help of a Latvian immigrant named Jacob Davis, Strauss made jeans a big business. Davis was a tailor. In the 1870s, he invented a new way to sew jeans. In addition to stitching seams with heavy thread, he added copper rivets. These short fasteners made jeans stronger than ever.

Many American workers adopted these tough trousers. Cowboys did wear them. But so did gold miners, factory employees, and off-duty soldiers in World War II.

In the 1950s, jeans came to symbolize rebellion. Actors such as James Dean and Marlon Brando wore jeans in films about young people who didn't want to follow society's rules.

Not everyone was happy about the style. Some restaurants and theaters would not let in people wearing jeans. Students were not allowed to wear them to school.

But within another decade or so, jeans had become more common. They are daily wear for many people in many parts of the world.

Fancy Pants

The most expensive pair of jeans ever sold was auctioned off in 2005 for sixty thousand dollars! They were Levi Strauss jeans that were more than 115 years old.

Levi Strauss started out supplying denim to miners in San Francisco in the 1850s.

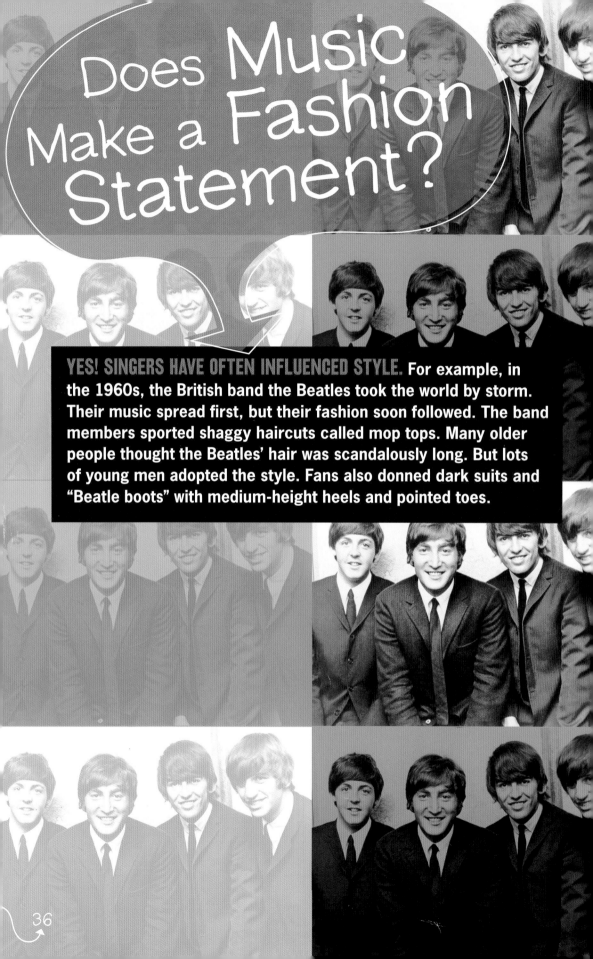

Does Music Make a Fashion Statement?

YES! SINGERS HAVE OFTEN INFLUENCED STYLE. For example, in the 1960s, the British band the Beatles took the world by storm. Their music spread first, but their fashion soon followed. The band members sported shaggy haircuts called mop tops. Many older people thought the Beatles' hair was scandalously long. But lots of young men adopted the style. Fans also donned dark suits and "Beatle boots" with medium-height heels and pointed toes.

Not long after the Beatles, another hot trend was punk. Like the Beatles, punk came from Britain. In the 1970s, young people were rebelling against society's norms. They rejected traditional ways of doing things. Punk rock bands such as the Clash and the Ramones wrote songs that reflected these ideas. The music was loud and thrashy, and the clothes were tight and trashy. Rather than wearing neat, new clothes, punks wore skintight, ripped jeans and torn shirts full of safety pins. They styled their hair into spiky dos called mohawks and pierced their ears and lips.

Beginning in the 1980s, hip-hop music became a big influence on fashion. Baggy pants, athletic shoes, sports jerseys, and flashy jewelry are common hip-hop styles. Many hip-hop stars, including Sean Combs (also known as Diddy), Jay-Z, and Eminem, have their own clothing lines.

The Ramones had a big impact on fashion in the 1970s.

In the 1990s, grunge was the fashion and the music of the moment. Many grunge bands, such as Nirvana, came from Seattle, Washington. And grunge fashion came from thrift stores. Flannel shirts, old jeans, and shaggy hair were grunge style standards.

The 2000s brought emo to the fashion world. Emo groups such as Panic at the Disco and Fall Out Boy sing emotional, sensitive songs. They and their fans sport long, floppy bangs; black clothing; and plenty of dark eyeliner.

These young people wear hip-hop fashions.

GLOSSARY

boater: a straw hat with a flat top and brim

chopine: a high platform shoe that some wealthy women in Venice, Italy, wore in the 1500s

corset: an undergarment that shapes the body

denim: a heavy cloth. Blue jeans are made of denim.

eating disorder: an illness that causes a person to adopt unhealthful eating habits, usually with the goal of weight loss. Anorexia and bulimia are eating disorders.

fedora: a men's hat with a curled brim and a creased crown

haute couture: high-quality fashion design. *Haute couture* means "high sewing" in French.

klompen: clunky wooden shoes worn in Holland in the 1200s

macaroni: a stylish British man of the 1700s

moccasin: a leather, slipperlike shoe traditionally worn by Native Americans

mohawk: a hairstyle in which most of the hair is shaved, except for a strip of hair from the middle of the forehead to the back of the neck

nautical mile: a unit used to measure distances at sea. One nautical mile is equal to 1.2 miles (1.9 km).

New Look: the nickname for a fashion line that French designer Christian Dior introduced in 1947

nylon: a strong but lightweight synthetic (man-made) fabric

poulaine: a men's shoe in fourteenth- and fifteenth-century Europe. Poulaines, also known as crackows, had long, pointy toes.

punk: a musical, social, and style movement that began in the 1970s. Punks rejected traditional social customs.

ration: to limit certain goods, often because there is a shortage

smelling salts: scented chemicals to revive a person who is feeling faint

supermodel: a famous and highly successful fashion model

taboo: against society's rules

vaquero: a Mexican cowboy

vogue: the fashion or style of a certain time. When something is in fashion, it can also be called in vogue.

SELECTED BIBLIOGRAPHY

Breward, Christopher. *Fashion.* New York: Oxford University Press, 2003.

Corson, Richard. *Fashions in Makeup: From Ancient to Modern Times.* New York: Universe Books, 1972.

Cumming, Valerie. *Understanding Fashion History.* Hollywood, CA: Costume and Fashion Press, 2004.

Leventon, Melissa. *What People Wore When: A Complete Illustrated History of Costume from Ancient Times to the Nineteenth Century for Every Level of Society.* New York: St. Martin's Griffin, 2008.

Peacock, John. *The Complete Fashion Sourcebook.* London: Thames & Hudson, 2005.

Phaidon Press. *The Fashion Book.* London: Phaidon Press, 1998.

Riordan, Teresa. *Inventing Beauty: A History of the Innovations That Have Made Us Beautiful.* New York: Broadway Books, 2004.

Tucker, Andrew, and Tamsin Kingswell. *Fashion: A Crash Course.* New York: Watson-Guptill Publications, 2000.

FURTHER READING

The Bata Shoe Museum
http://www.batashoemuseum.ca
This museum, based in Toronto, Canada, holds thousands of shoes from all over the world and all time periods. Its website offers a glimpse of this amazing collection.

Beker, Jeanne. *Passion for Fashion: Careers in Style.* Toronto: Tundra Books, 2008. If you have a passion for fashion, let Jeanne Beker—a fashion writer and actress—tell you about ways you can make it your career.

Bertoletti, John C. *How Fashion Designers Use Math.* New York: Chelsea Clubhouse, 2010. Perfect for aspiring fashion designers, this book tells all about how math is connected to fashion careers.

Fashion Passion Homepage
http://library.thinkquest.org/19760/home.html
Check out this site for interesting information on fashion and designers. Click on the "Decades" link for a look at fashion trends from the early 1900s to the 1990s.

Krohn, Katherine. *Vera Wang: Enduring Style.* Minneapolis: Twenty-First Century Books, 2009. Vera Wang is a talented and well-known fashion designer. Learn more about her life and work in this book!

MacDonald, Fiona. *Everyday Clothes through History.* Milwaukee: Gareth Stevens, 2007. Learn more about what kinds of clothes people have worn over the years and why.

Sills, Leslie. *From Rags to Riches: A History of Girls' Clothing in America.* New York: Holiday House, 2005. Take a look at how styles have changed for girls in the United States over the years.

INDEX

ACKNOWLEDGMENTS
The images in this book are used with the permission of:
© Geoff Brightling/Dorling Kindersley/Getty Images, pp. 1,
6–7; Library of Congress, pp. 2 (top, LC-USZ62-101143), 9
(LC-USZ62-101143), 29 (bottom, LC-DIG-nclc-00069), 31 (top,
LC-DIG-ppmsc-05799); © JGI/Jamie Grill/Blend Images/Getty
Images, p. 2 (bottom); © Thinkstock/Comstock Images/Getty
Images, pp. 3, 28–29; © Mark Mainz/Getty Images, pp. 4, 32;
© Dat/Dreamstime.com, p. 5; © London Stereoscopic
Company/Hulton Archive/Getty Images, p. 5 (inset); The Art
Archive/Bill Manns, p. 7 (inset); © Andreas Kuehn/
Photographer's Choice/Getty Images, p. 8; © Jon Gray/Stone/
Getty Images, pp. 10–11; © Topham/The Image Works,
pp. 12–13; © G.W. Hales/Hulton Archive/Getty Images, p. 12
(inset); © gulfimages/Getty Images, p. 14; © Alfred Eisenstaedt/
Time & Life Pictures/Getty Images, p. 15; © Tim Graham/The
Image Bank/Getty Images, p. 16; © Stockbyte/Getty Images,
p. 17 (top); © Frank Zeller/AFP/Getty Images, p. 17 (bottom);
© Bettmann/CORBIS, p. 18; © Image Source/Getty Images,
pp. 19, 22–23; © Michael Blann/Stone/Getty Images,
pp. 20–21; © David Young-Wolff/Alamy, p. 21 (top); © Jon
Arnold Images Ltd/Alamy, p. 21 (bottom); The Art Archive, p. 22
(inset); The Granger Collection, New York, p. 23 (inset); © China
Photos/Getty Images, p. 24; The Art Archive/Private Collection/
Marc Charmet, p. 25; © WILDLIFE Gmbh/Alamy, pp. 26–27;
© iStockphoto.com/Don Nichols, p. 27 (top); © Scott
Camazine/Alamy, p. 27 (bottom); © Britt Erlanson/Cultura/
Photolibrary, p. 29 (top); The Art Archive/Museo Correr Venice/
Gianni Dagli Orti, p. 30; © Marilyn Angel Wynn/Nativestock.com/
Getty Images, p. 31 (bottom); AP Photo/Matt Dunham, p. 33;
© Marc Romanelli/The Image Bank/Getty Images, pp. 34–35;
AP Photo, p. 35 (inset); © Michael Ochs Archives/Getty Images,
pp. 36, 37 (top); © Janine Wiedel Photolibrary/Alamy, p. 37
(bottom).

Front Cover: © Gary Cralle/Photographer's Choice/Getty Images
(hat); © iStockphoto.com/Tomislav Stajduhar (water).

Text copyright © 2011 by Alison Behnke
Illustrations © 2011 by Lerner Publishing Group, Inc.

Lerner Publications Company
A division of Lerner Publishing Group, Inc.
241 First Avenue North
Minneapolis, MN 55401 U.S.A.

Website address: www.lernerbooks.com

Library of Congress Cataloging-in-Publication Data

Behnke, Allison
    Does a ten-gallon hat really hold ten gallons? : and other
questions about fashion / by Alison Behnke.
        p.   cm. — (Is that a fact?)
    Includes bibliographical references and index.
    ISBN 978-0-7613-4913-6 (lib. bdg. : alk. paper)
    1. Health—Miscellanea. I. Title.
TT507.B419 2011
746.9'2—dc22   2009027452

Manufactured in the United States of America
1 – CG – 7/15/2010